mm

★ ★ ★ IT'S MY STATE! ★ ★ ★ ★ ★

MASSACHUSETTS

Ruth Bjorklund

Stephanie Fitzgerald

mc **Marshall Cavendish**
Benchmark
New York

Published by Marshall Cavendish Benchmark
An imprint of Marshall Cavendish Corporation

Website: www.marshallcavendish.us

This publication represents the opinions and views of the authors based on their personal experience, knowledge, and research. The information in this book serves as a general guide only. The authors and publisher have used their best efforts in preparing this book and disclaim liability rising directly and indirectly from the use and application of this book.

Other Marshall Cavendish Offices:
Marshall Cavendish International (Asia) Private Limited, 1 New Industrial Road, Singapore 536196 •
Marshall Cavendish International (Thailand) Co Ltd. 253 Asoke, 12th Flr, Sukhumvit 21 Road, Klongtoey Nua,
Wattana, Bangkok 10110, Thailand • Marshall Cavendish (Malaysia) Sdn Bhd, Times Subang, Lot 46, Subang
Hi-Tech Industrial Park, Batu Tiga, 40000 Shah Alam, Selangor Darul Ehsan, Malaysia

Marshall Cavendish is a trademark of Times Publishing Limited

All websites were available and accurate when this book was sent to press.

Library of Congress Cataloging-in-Publication Data
Bjorklund, Ruth.
        Massachusetts / Ruth Bjorklund, Stephanie Fitzgerald. — 2nd ed.
            p. cm. — (It's my state)
        Includes index.
        ISBN 978-1-60870-053-0
        1. Massachusetts—Juvenile literature. I. Fitzgerald, Stephanie. II. Title.
    F64.3.B57 2011
    974.4—dc22   2010003927

Second Edition developed for Marshall Cavendish Benchmark by RJF Publishing LLC (www.RJFpublishing.com)
Series Designer, Second Edition: Tammy West/Westgraphix LLC
Editor, Second Edition: Emily Dolbear

All maps, illustrations, and graphics © Marshall Cavendish Corporation. Maps and artwork on pages 6, 32, 33, 75, and back cover by Christopher Santoro. Map and graphics on pages 8 and 44 by Westgraphix LLC. Map on page 76 by Mapping Specialists.

The photographs in this book are used by permission and through the courtesy of:
Front cover: Steve Elmore/Getty Images and GoGo Images Corporation/Alamy (inset).
Alamy: Ilene MacDonald, 12; Chris Pancewicz, 13; Paul Mozell, 14; Alan Haynes, 15; Photos 12, 20; Ivy Close Images, 26; North Wind Picture Archives, 34, 36; Ball Miwako, 40; Della Huff, 42; Eric Fowke, 51; Michael Dwyer, 53; National Geographic Image Collection, 62; Ruben Kincaid, 66; Pictorial Press Ltd , 69; Yakoniva, 74. *AP Images:* Steven Senne, 57; Nancy Palmieri, 58; CHITOSE SUZUKI, 61. *Corbis:* 38; David H. Wells, 43. *Getty Images:* GK Hart/Vikki Hart, 4; Matthew O'Shea, 5 (bottom); Dirk Anschutz, 9; David Lyons, 10; Michael Springer, 11, 23; Stephen Frink, 18 (top); Dorling Kindersley, 18 (bottom); De Agostini, 19; Stock Montage, 22; SSPL, 24; MPI/Stringer/Hulton Archives, 28; FPG, 29; Hulton Archive, 31, 46 (top); Topical Press Agency/Hulton Archive, 37; Herbert Orth/Time & Life Pictures, 46 (bottom); Jordan Strauss/WireImage, 47; Lee Lockwood//Time & Life Pictures, 50; Brian Ach/WireImage, 52; Andrew McCaul, 67; Blank Archives, 68; Lisa Valder, 70 (top); Ross M Horowitz, 70 (bottom); Steve Dunwell Photography Inc, 71; Scott Olson, 73. *Shutterstock:* teekaygee, 5 (top); Mary Lane, 44; Chee-Onn Leong, 45; Jorge Salcedo, 48; Roux Frederic, 60; Bill Perry, 64; Christopher Penler, 72. *U.S. Fish and Wildlife Service:* 16; 17.

Printed in Malaysia (T).
135642

CONTENTS

A Quick Look at Massachusetts...................................4

1 The Bay State 7

　Massachusetts Counties Map................................8

　Plants & Animals 18

2 From the Beginning 21

　Making Hand-Dipped Candles 32

　Important Dates 39

3 The People..41

　Who Massachusettsans Are 44

　Famous Bay Staters.......................................46

　Calendar of Events 52

4 How the Government Works...............................55

　Branches of Government 56

5 Making a Living 63

　Workers & Industries......................................65

　Recipe for Cranberry Sauce 67

　Products & Resources 70

State Flag & Seal 75

Massachusetts State Map 76

State Song 77

More About Massachusetts 78

Index...79

State Flower: Mayflower

The mayflower has sweet-smelling pink or white petals and grows in the sandy and rocky soil of the state's woodlands. The mayflower has had protected status in the state since 1925.

State Dog: Boston Terrier

A cross between an English bulldog and an English terrier, the Boston terrier was the first purebred dog developed in the United States.

State Tree: American Elm

The American elm was adopted as the state tree to honor General George Washington, who took command of the Continental Army beneath an elm in Cambridge Common in 1775. This large tree with gray, flaky bark has dark green oval leaves that turn yellow in fall.

State Marine Mammal: Right Whale

Whalers considered this mammal the "right," or best, whale to hunt for its blubber, which was used to produce lamp oil. Early New Englanders hunted this whale, which swims closer to shore than most other whales, almost into extinction. Today, many people work together to protect this highly endangered species.

State Bird: Black-Capped Chickadee

The black-capped chickadee is one of the most familiar North American birds. This tiny flyer is only about 5 inches (13 centimeters) long, including its tail, which accounts for half its length. The gray, brown, black, and white bird often nests in stumps, in trees, or on fence posts. It is easily identified by its song—"chick-adee-dee-dee."

State Cookie: Chocolate Chip Cookie

In 1930, Ruth Wakefield, the owner of the Toll House Inn in Whitman, Massachusetts, tried mixing pieces of semisweet chocolate into her dough for butter cookies. Her "toll house" chocolate chip cookies became famous throughout the state as well as the nation.

MASSACHUSETTS

Berkshires

Quabbin
Reservoir

Harvard
University

Cambridge

New England Aquarium

Springfield

Old Sturbridge
Village

Boston

Cape Cod

Basketball
Hall of
Fame

Plymouth
Rock

1620

Connecticutt River

Martha's
Vineyard

Nantucket Island

N

W   E

S

Atlantic Ocean

The Bay State

People say the name *Massachusetts* comes from the language of the Massachuset tribe. The words *massa* (great) and *wachusetts* (mountain) together mean Great Mountain Place.

Massachusetts is part of New England, a region in the northeastern part of the country that also includes Connecticut, Rhode Island, Vermont, New Hampshire, and Maine. Massachusetts contains fourteen counties. Boston, the state's capital and largest city, is part of Suffolk County in the eastern part of the state.

At just 7,840 square miles (20,306 square kilometers), Massachusetts is a small state, but it has a wide variety of landforms. In fact, it has more than any other New England state. Massachusetts has many types of beaches—some are sandy and flat; others are rocky and steep. Rivers flow throughout the state, including New England's largest, the Connecticut River. There are mountain ranges, rolling farmlands, sand dunes, swamps, lakes, and forests.

Western Massachusetts

The scenic Berkshire Hills in western Massachusetts is a great place to enjoy the brilliant colors of fall. Hardwood trees such as oak, beech, maple, and white birch

Quick Facts

MASSACHUSETTS BORDERS

North	Vermont
	New Hampshire
South	Connecticut
	Rhode Island
East	Atlantic Ocean
West	New York

Massachusetts Counties

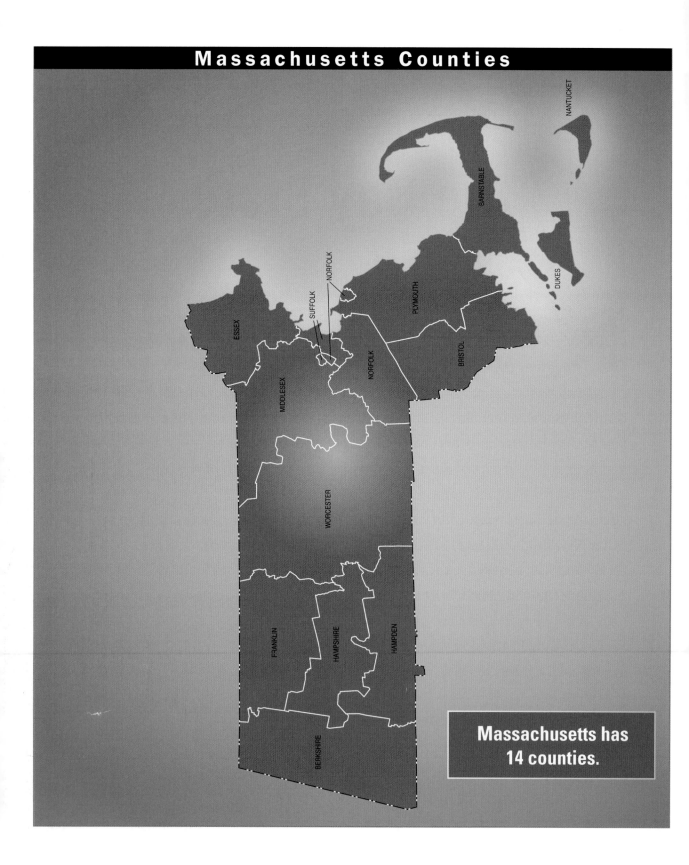

NANTUCKET

BARNSTABLE

DUKES

NORFOLK

SUFFOLK

PLYMOUTH

ESSEX

NORFOLK

BRISTOL

MIDDLESEX

WORCESTER

FRANKLIN

HAMPSHIRE

HAMPDEN

BERKSHIRE

Massachusetts has 14 counties.

MOTHER AND DAUGHTER FALLS

The most scenic waterfall in the Berkshires is called Bash Bish Falls. It splits in two before dropping about 50 feet (15 meters) into a pool of blue water. Some people say the water makes a "bash-bish" sound as it hits the pool. Others tell a Mahican legend about a beautiful Indian woman named Bash-Bish. She angered her husband, so he tied her to a canoe and sent her over the falls. Then, Bash-Bish's grieving daughter jumped into the waterfall to join her. At night, when the moon shines on the pool, people say they can see the faces of the women over the water.

cover the hills. When the weather cools, the leaves turn many shades of yellow, red, and gold.

When it was first formed, the Berkshire mountain range featured sharp and jagged peaks. After millions of years, however, wind, ice, and water wore away the peaks. Eventually, they were worn down to only the hardest rock, creating the rounded hills that exist today. Because the ground is rugged and the soil is poor, few people have farmed this region, where beavers, bobcats,

Beautiful Bash Bish Falls is the highest single-drop waterfall in Massachusetts.

wild turkeys, snowshoe hares, porcupines, black bears, and mink live. Nearby are two large river valleys, the Hoosic and the Housatonic. These valleys feature wonderful white-water rapids, waterfalls, and sheer walls of marble, quartz, and granite. Mount Greylock, the state's highest peak, rises here. The mountain reaches 3,491 feet (1,064 m) at its summit.

The Connecticut River Valley

The Connecticut River runs north to south for 68 miles (109 km) through the center of Massachusetts. The river flows by fertile farms, wetlands, dinosaur-footprint fossils, and a 300-million-year-old lava flow. Not far from the Connecticut River is a valuable natural resource called Quabbin Reservoir. In the 1930s, Boston and other big cities wanted to dam a river because they needed more fresh water. Officials asked the citizens of four nearby towns to relocate. They agreed, and their houses and businesses were moved by truck. Workers built a dam, which helped flood the abandoned towns. Today, migrating birds along with deer, coyotes, and eagles flock to Quabbin Reservoir. This wildlife refuge is full of color in spring, when thousands of dragonflies and butterflies gather.

Mount Greylock State Reservation, created in 1898, is Massachusetts's first wilderness state park.

Eastern Massachusetts

Although Eastern Massachusetts is the most populated area of the state, it has lots of natural places to explore. Along the North Shore, birders come from all over the world to watch for the thousands of shorebirds that live in the marshes, sand dunes, and wetlands. The fishing communities of Gloucester and Rockport are located on Cape Ann, which juts into the sea. From Cape Ann to north of Boston, the coastline is rocky, with many small islands. Boston and its far-reaching suburbs are built along the shores of Boston Harbor. Two major rivers, the Mystic and the Charles, flow into the harbor. During the last Ice Age, which ended about 11,500 years ago, glaciers covered the coastline from what is now Boston to Cape Cod, carving out ponds, rock ledges, and river valleys. When Earth's climate warmed, the glaciers drew back, leaving behind small rocks and giant boulders. The most famous of these boulders is Plymouth Rock.

Quick Facts

NO ORDINARY ROCK

According to legend, Plymouth Rock is where the Pilgrims first landed in 1620. Today, the rock is housed in Massachusetts's smallest state park, Pilgrim Memorial State Park. Every year about one million tourists come to Plymouth Rock, making it the most visited rock in New England.

Visitors look over a railing at Plymouth Rock in Pilgrim Memorial State Park.

Cape Cod

American nature writer Henry David Thoreau called Cape Cod "the bare and bended arm of Massachusetts." Cape Cod, located at the easternmost part of Massachusetts, stretches 65 miles (105 km) into the Atlantic Ocean. All along the Cape, there are forests, swamps, salt marshes, sandy beaches, cliffs, and dunes. The outward side of the "arm" faces east to the Atlantic. Tides and storms pound the shoreline, pushing the sand into fantastic shapes. A series of islands, including Nantucket, Martha's Vineyard, and the Elizabeth Islands, lie to the south in Nantucket Sound. On the inside of the "arm's" curve, salt marshes and cranberry bogs line the shores of Cape Cod Bay.

The Four Seasons

It is not only the landscape in Massachusetts that offers a lot of variety. Residents of this New England state enjoy a full range of seasons—winter, spring, summer, and fall. "I truly think the most beautiful part of the country

President John F. Kennedy created the Cape Cod National Seashore in 1961. It has more than 43,000 acres (17,400 hectares) of beaches, ponds, and woods.

MOBILE LIGHTHOUSE

Beginning in 1797, the first lighthouse that Boston-bound ocean travelers saw was the Highland Light, or Cape Cod Light. It stood 500 feet (152 m) from the ocean's edge atop a cliff at the end of Cape Cod. But centuries of powerful winter storms, or nor'easters, eroded the beach so that by 1990, the lighthouse was only 100 feet (30 m) from the edge. In 1996, Cape residents, afraid the lighthouse would topple into the sea, moved it inland.

Highland Light, or Cape Cod Light, now stands near Truro.

is here. We have great winters, wonderful summers, mountains, the shore, and Cape Cod. It is unique," says a proud resident.

In summer, Massachusetts has even temperatures. Many summer days are humid and sticky. In fall, days are cool and crisp, with clear blue skies. Leaves turn dazzling colors. When winter sets in, nights grow long, and the average temperature drops to 30 degrees Fahrenheit (1 degree Celsius). Lakes and ponds freeze over, and snowfall can be as much as 67 inches (170 cm) a year in the colder mountainous areas. Spring is the shortest season. There may be frost on the ground as late as May.

Year-round, the ocean affects the climate along the coast. On a hot summer day, beachgoers enjoy cool breezes from the sea. In winter, coastal temperatures are usually warmer than inland. But nor'easters can roar across the North Atlantic Ocean and hit the beach with terrific force. Nor'easters blast coastal towns with heavy snowfalls and fallen trees, causing floods and power outages.

A nor'easter, a strong storm that causes the waters to grow very rough, strikes the coast of Nahant.

Wildlife and Water

Massachusetts features thousands of miles of seashore and riverbanks, as well as many wetlands, lakes, and ponds. Average rainfall in the state is 44 inches (112 cm), which is enough to keep most swamps, marshes, and rivers from going dry. These areas have long been home to a variety of Massachusetts's wildlife.

Since the 1860s, factories and towns have crowded the shores and riverbanks of the state's waterways. Waste from homes and factories has polluted rivers, lakes, streams, harbors, bays, and the ocean itself. Over time, many native species have died off completely, while others have become threatened or endangered. In 1988, President George H. W. Bush called Boston Harbor "the filthiest harbor in America." But Massachusetts residents took charge. After a multibillion-dollar cleanup effort, Boston Harbor is no longer an oozing, smelly mess. The water is cleaner. Native fish species are back, and sea life is healthier. Swimmers, boaters, and beachcombers have returned.

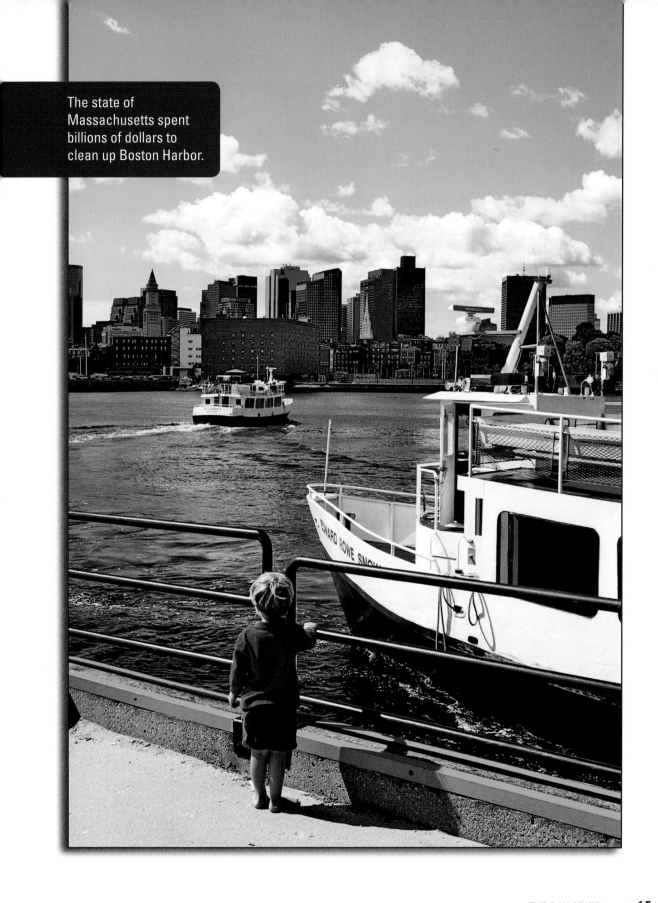

The state of Massachusetts spent billions of dollars to clean up Boston Harbor.

Today's citizens are also working to repair damage to the wild areas of Cape Cod. Early settlers, the Pilgrims, created Cape Cod's famous dunes when they cut down the trees for

pastureland. Crashing waves and strong winds turned the treeless land into a sandy, desertlike place. At first, the sand was in danger of washing away. But beach grasses grew, holding the sand in place and protecting the habitats of the Cape's creatures—red foxes, coyotes, great horned owls, marsh hawks, blue herons, hognose snakes, herring gulls, and piping plovers. Still, some beach dwellers continue to be at risk.

The U.S. government lists the piping plover, a tiny bird, as threatened in Massachusetts. (People must take special steps to protect threatened or endangered plants and animals.) Cape Cod residents have closed off sections of beach where the plovers make their nests. Thanks to these efforts, the piping plover population is growing.

Another endangered species is the northern red-bellied cooter, formerly known as the Plymouth redbelly turtle. This reptile has trouble sharing its home with human neighbors. Redbellies live mainly in ponds but nest in forests and meadows. As human populations have increased, the turtles have

The piping plovers of Massachusetts need protection to survive.

lost protected nesting sites. The turtles' eggs—and tiny hatchlings—are especially vulnerable to predators such as skunks and raccoons. Predators destroy as many as half the cooters' nests each year.

In 1980, the Natural Heritage and Endangered Species Program (part of the Massachusetts Division of Fisheries and Wildlife) began a special effort to save the northern red-bellied cooter. Each fall, biologists collect about one hundred hatchlings from their nests. They raise the tiny baby turtles in captivity for the first year and then release the turtles into the wild. Thanks to this special treatment, the yearlings are the size of three-year-old turtles when they are set free. Large cooters are less likely to be preyed on and have a better chance of surviving to adulthood.

Plants & Animals

American Beaver

For thousands of years, beavers were an important part of New England's ecology. They gnawed young trees to build lodges and dams in Massachusetts's many streams, lakes, and ponds. However, years of intensive trapping, combined with loss of habitat, caused the beaver to disappear from the state from the late 1700s to the early 1900s. After an effort to restore beavers to the region, populations were up again by the 1950s.

Humpback Whale

The acrobatic—and endangered—humpback whale is a favorite among Massachusetts's whale-watchers. Humpbacks can grow to 60 feet (18 m) long, weigh up to 40 tons (36,000 kilograms), and eat about 5,000 pounds (2,300 kg) of plankton, krill, and fish a day! Though it is hard to tell, no two whales are alike. Each has a different pattern on its fluke, or tail.

Huckleberry

A tasty ingredient in pies and muffins, the huckleberry is also a treat for bears and the caterpillars that turn into butterflies. Henry David Thoreau once wrote, "This crop grows wild all over the country, wholesome, bountiful, and free, a real ambrosia."

Snowy Tree Cricket

On summer evenings, the male snowy tree cricket chirps loudly to attract a mate. This critter is also called the "thermometer cricket" because a person can estimate the temperature by counting its chirps. Simply count the number of chirps you hear in a thirteen-second interval and add forty to get the current temperature in Fahrenheit.

Spotted Salamander

Spotted salamanders live in Massachusetts's hardwood forests. In early spring, at the first warm rain, they come out of the ground and travel to pools, where they breed. Unfortunately, human-made obstacles, such as roadways, pose a major threat. State environmentalists have created special tunnels to help the salamanders cross under roadways. They also close certain roads during breeding season.

White Oak Tree

For many, the white oak tree represents strength, power, stateliness, and grace. In colonial times, people often gathered to meet, teach, or sign important documents under the protective branches of a tall oak. The decks of Massachusetts's most powerful warship, the USS *Constitution* (also known as *Old Ironsides*), were made of white oak.

From the Beginning

Many millions of years ago, what we now call Massachusetts was a warm rain forest, full of dinosaurs and other prehistoric creatures. In other periods of the state's geologic history, the climate was much colder. In these ice-age periods, the land was buried beneath a thick layer of ice. When the last Ice Age ended about 11,500 years ago, plants and animals again thrived in the area, and exciting things began to happen.

The First People

The first people who lived in present-day Massachusetts arrived there about 11,000 years ago. They made stone weapons for hunting and gathered nuts and berries from the forests and shellfish from the beaches. About two thousand to three thousand years ago, several Algonquian-speaking tribes settled along the streams and rivers of what is now Massachusetts. They began to form semipermanent villages. The people lived in lodges and wigwams, which they made by stretching tree bark and animal

Quick Facts

THE REAL BIG FOOT?
The fossilized footprints of a 200-million-year-old theropod dinosaur have been found in Granby, Massachusetts. The creature measured 50 feet (15 m) from head to tail.

This illustration shows an Algonquian Indian village from 1585.

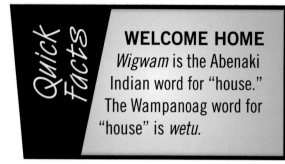
hides over wooden frames. They grew crops, hunted, and fished, moving with the seasons to take advantage of different food sources. Algonquian tribes living near the sea caught fish and hunted whales. Those living on Cape Cod were called the Nausets. Other Algonquians were the Patuxet, Wampanoag, and Nipmuc tribes.

Europeans Arrive

Historians believe that about a thousand years ago, Norse explorers might have been the first Europeans to view the lands that would become Massachusetts. About five hundred years went by before other European explorers reached what is now New England. The Italian explorer Giovanni da Verrazzano surveyed the northeast coast of North America in 1524. In the next century, John Smith (who had founded the Jamestown colony in Virginia in 1607) gave New England its name after he mapped the area from Penobscot Bay, in present-day Maine, to Cape Cod in 1614.

During the early 1600s, unrest was growing in England. The Church of England had

After founding the Jamestown colony in Virginia, John Smith explored the northeast coast.

A Pilgrim portrayer chats with real Wampanoag Indians in traditional dress at today's Plimoth Plantation, a living-history museum.

become very powerful and forbade people to practice other religions. Some people opposed to the Church of England became known as Separatists, and some of them decided to leave.

On September 16, 1620, a group of 102 Separatists (now known as Pilgrims) and other English people set sail for America aboard a ship named the *Mayflower*. The two-month sea journey was horrid. The Pilgrims had been granted territory in Virginia, but the *Mayflower* strayed off course, and the newcomers came ashore at Cape Cod. After attempts to reach a destination in New York failed, they decided to stay near where they first landed. They wrote an agreement called the Mayflower Compact. In it, they promised to govern themselves and to make only fair and just laws "for ye generall good of ye Colonie."

The first Pilgrim settlement was a coastal village they called Plimoth (spelled *Plymouth* today). The Pilgrims knew that a cold winter would soon be upon them, so they quickly built homes using poles and grasses. Wild animals lurked in the woods, and the native people made the Pilgrims uneasy. Yet they were pleasantly surprised to find fields ready for planting. It gave them hope for spring.

In this engraving, the Pilgrims meet Chief Massasoit and other Wampanoags for the first time.

The Wampanoag tribe and their chief, Massasoit, watched the newcomers carefully. Finally, the chief sent a messenger named Samoset, who arrived at Plymouth and said simply, "Welcome, English." (Samoset had probably learned some of the language from Englishmen who came to fish off the coast of what is now northern New England and Canada.) The Pilgrims were excited to find someone who spoke their language and eagerly began to ask him questions. They wondered why there were fields ready for planting but no people in the area. Samoset told them the tilled fields belonged to the Patuxets, a tribe whose members had all died from disease. After Samoset brought his report back to Massasoit, the chief and his attendants visited Plymouth. Though there was little trust between the two groups, the Wampanoags and the Pilgrims signed the first peace treaty between Europeans and American Indians. It lasted for more than fifty years.

One member of Chief Masassoit's party was a man named Tisquantum, or Squanto. He was the last remaining Patuxet. He spoke English because he had once lived in England as a slave. Squanto wanted to live on his ancestors' land and decided to help the Pilgrims. He taught them how to grow corn, where to hunt and fish, and which berries and nuts were good to eat. Thanks to Squanto, the Pilgrims were able to survive their first year in the new land and harvest a crop. For three days after the harvest, the Pilgrims and Massasoit's tribe celebrated an English feast called Harvest Home, which Americans now call Thanksgiving. In the following years, the Pilgrims' colony grew in size as more people came from England and several new towns were established.

> ## In Their Own Words
>
> *[Massasoit] was a chief renowned more in peace than war, and was, as long as he lived, a friend to the English, notwithstanding they committed repeated [forceful seizure] upon his lands and liberties.*
>
> —Samuel Drake, a historian, 1832

The Massachusetts Bay Colony

In 1628, the first members of another religious group—the Puritans—arrived in the area. They joined an existing small settlement that was later named Salem. In 1630, a much larger group of Puritans arrived and soon settled nearby in what is now Boston to establish the Massachusetts Bay Colony.

The Puritans built small villages surrounding a section of open land called a commons. They farmed nearby fields in warm weather and made useful things, such as furniture, farm tools, horse harnesses, and clothing, in winter. The Puritans were stern people who believed in simple living and hard work.

New settlers continued to arrive from England, and the Massachusetts settlements grew. In 1691, England combined the Plymouth and Massachusetts Bay colonies into the single colony of Massachusetts.

The Dark Days

In many ways, life was difficult in seventeenth-century Massachusetts. The Puritans were powerful and often forced their beliefs on others. Puritan farmers and American Indians fought bitterly over land. Many colony members did not trust one another. In 1692, when two girls in Salem fell sick seemingly without cause, the so-called Dark Days began. The girls fainted, had seizures, and slept little. A doctor declared them bewitched, a condition punishable by hanging. The girls blamed a slave named Tituba, saying, "She afflicts me! She comes to me at night and torments me! She's a witch!"

Nineteen people were hanged during the Salem witch trials. As many as seventeen others may have died in prison.

Soon, people all over Salem were accusing each other of witchcraft. Most of the accused were unmarried or widowed women who owned farmland. Many historians think that the accusers wanted the women's property. A court was set up to hear the witchcraft cases. In less than a year, more than 150 people were sent to prison. By the time the "Witchcraft Court" was shut down, nineteen people had been hanged and one person had been pressed to death under heavy stones.

The Salem witchcraft trials marked a troubled time in Massachusetts's history, as did the struggle over land between the American Indians and the English colonists. In 1675, Massasoit's son, King Philip, tried to keep the English off tribal land and declared war. (His real name was Metacom. King Philip was the name English settlers gave him.) After two years of brutal fighting, Philip was killed in battle. Many of his Indian supporters fled to Canada or the American West. Others stayed and adopted English ways.

Wars and Taxes

King Philip's War, as it was called, was not the only land conflict the colonists— or the English—faced in America. Fur traders and settlers from France had also come to eastern North America. In the 1600s and 1700s, France and Great Britain fought several wars for control of eastern North America and its valuable natural resources. The French and Indian War (1754–1763) was the largest of these conflicts. Great Britain won the war, but the victory came at a great price. The British government had borrowed a great deal of money to pay for the war, and it needed to keep British troops in North America.

To help raise money to pay off the country's debt, King George III and the British Parliament began imposing new taxes on the colonies. The king was also eager to regain control over colonial governments that had been acting more and more independently while Britain was distracted by its wars. The British government wanted its American colonies to trade only with Britain, but many people in Massachusetts wanted to be free to trade with other countries too.

Several new taxes and other actions by the British government, starting in 1763, angered the colonists. When the first of the Townshend Acts was passed in 1767, many colonists had had enough. The Townshend Acts put new taxes on many kinds of imported goods. Many colonists did not feel they should have to pay taxes imposed by a government in which they had no voice. Colonists who opposed the actions of the British government became known as patriots. Their battle cry became, "No taxation without representation!"

On December 16, 1773, colonists dumped 342 containers of tea into Boston Harbor to protest British taxation.

The seeds for independence had been sown, and they flowered first in Massachusetts. On March 5, 1770, British soldiers opened fire on colonial protesters in an attack later known as the Boston Massacre. Five people were killed. Later, to oppose the British government's tax on tea, a group of colonists known as the Sons of Liberty organized a protest called the Boston Tea Party. One night in 1773, the protesters sneaked aboard a ship full of English tea in Boston Harbor and threw the tea overboard. In 1774, the British government passed a series of laws that became known in the colonies as the Intolerable Acts. One of the measures was to close the port of Boston.

Soon British soldiers, or "regulars," wearing red coats were everywhere. Farmers put down their plows for guns. They called themselves minutemen because it was said they could prepare for battle in just one minute. When British soldiers planned to march on the towns of Lexington and Concord (outside Boston) to capture patriot leaders and seize weapons, a group of patriots discovered their plan. Boston silversmith Paul Revere secretly rowed across the Charles River, and he and two other men then journeyed on horseback through the countryside to warn the minutemen that the British were coming.

Paul Revere's ride to alert colonists that British troops were on the march is one of the best-known stories from the American Revolution.

An American Revolution

On April 19, 1775, minutemen and British regulars confronted each other at Lexington. It is not known for certain who fired the first shot—what poet Ralph Waldo Emerson later called "the shot heard 'round the world"—but the first fighting of the American Revolution took place at Lexington that day. From Lexington, the British went on to Concord, where they battled again with minutemen. As the British retreated back to Boston, colonial forces repeatedly shot at them. At the end of the day's fighting, some 250 British soldiers were dead or wounded, and about 90 Americans had been killed or injured. The military consequences were not great, but the outcome gave the colonists hope. They had managed to embarrass the better equipped, better trained—and more respected—British army.

After the battles of Lexington and Concord, the British soldiers stayed in Boston, and reinforcements arrived in May. In June, American forces were sent to Charlestown Peninsula, across the Charles River from Boston, to occupy Bunker Hill. They ended up building fortifications on nearby Breed's Hill. British soldiers tried to storm the fortifications and were pushed back twice, suffering heavy losses. The American forces, low on ammunition, fled when the British regulars made their third charge.

More than one thousand British troops and about four hundred Americans were killed or wounded during the Battle of Bunker Hill. Although the colonists had been pushed back, they still encircled the British in Boston. Months later, in March 1776, General George Washington took control of colonial troops around Boston. His forces occupied and put cannons on Dorchester Heights, a line of hills south of Boston that overlooked the city. British general William Howe soon realized he was in the middle of enemy territory occupying a city that he could not defend. On March 17, 1776, the British army left Boston for good.

Declaring Independence

A few months later, on July 4, 1776, the Continental Congress—representatives of all the colonies meeting in Philadelphia—adopted the Declaration of

Independence. Of course, declaring independence does not make it so. For the next seven years, the colonists continued to battle British soldiers throughout the Thirteen Colonies. By the time the Treaty of Paris ended the war in 1783, with Great Britain recognizing American independence, it is estimated that more than 25,000 American soldiers had died for the cause.

In Massachusetts, John Adams and other leaders wrote a constitution for the Commonwealth of Massachusetts. (The first draft was called a Constitution for the State of Massachusetts, but people rejected it.) The document included rules for a new government that was based on democracy and citizens' rights—which did not include rights for women and slaves. It was a model for the U.S. Constitution and the Bill of Rights. In 1788, Massachusetts became the sixth state to ratify the U.S. Constitution.

British military forces reach the top of Breed's Hill, where they clash with colonial troops during the Battle of Bunker Hill in 1775.

MAKING HAND-DIPPED CANDLES

Although store-bought goods were available, many colonists used homemade items, such as tools, clothing, and candles. Because they provided the main source of light, candles were essential. You can make a hand-dipped candle much as the colonists did. Be sure to ask an adult for help with this project.

You will need these materials from a hardware or crafts supply store:

Candle wicking

Metal washers

Paraffin

Stearic acid

WHAT YOU WILL NEED

Water

2 tall cans

Large skillet

Stove

Candy thermometer

Stick

To Make the Wick

Braid two or three strands of wicking together. (Hint: A wick that is too fat will make your candle smoke, and a wick that is too thin will make the flame go out.) Cut the braided strand to a length 4 inches (10 cm) longer than the candle you want to make. Form a loop at one end of the strand and tie a metal washer to the other end (to weigh it down). Thread the looped end of the wick onto a stick.

To Make the Candle

Fill one can 3/4 to the top with paraffin. If you add 3 tablespoons (44 milliliters) of stearic acid per pound of paraffin, your candles will burn better. Fill the other can 3/4 with water. Fill the skillet 1/2 full of water and place it over low heat. Stand the can of paraffin in the skillet.

Melt the paraffin to about 160°F (71°C). Use the thermometer to make sure the temperature remains fairly steady—and be careful! The melted wax might not look hot, but it can burn you. With help from an adult, hold the stick with the wicking attached, and dip it into the wax. Continue dipping, alternating each dip into the wax with a dip into the water, until your candle reaches the desired thickness. Cut the bottom of the candle to remove the washer—and make the bottom flat—and snip the looped end of the wick to 1/2 inch (1.25 cm).

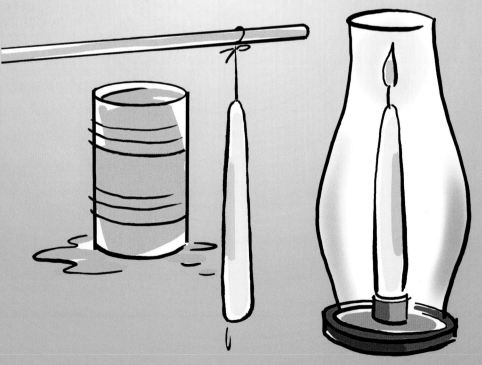

Revolutionary Ideas

In the nineteenth century, Massachusetts played a major role in another revolution—the Industrial Revolution. There had been manufacturing in Massachusetts since the mid–1600s, but the state did not become a powerhouse in the industry until about two hundred years later. In 1814, a Massachusetts resident named Francis Cabot Lowell built a loom in Waltham that ran by waterpower. A loom is a device that weaves thread into cloth. Lowell had visited a cotton mill in England, where he closely examined the workings of a power loom. Before he built his first mill with a water-powered loom, American looms were operated by hand. A water-powered loom can weave cloth much more quickly than a hand-operated one. Another one of Lowell's mills transformed the town of Lowell into the nation's first major manufacturing city. The Industrial Revolution had come to Massachusetts.

The young women who worked in Lowell's textile factories in the 1850s were known as Lowell Mill Girls.

Cities such as Lawrence, Fall River, and New Bedford soon had large factories for making textiles (cloth), taking advantage of the waterpower in the state's rivers. By the end of the nineteenth century, Massachusetts produced more than a third of the nation's wool and cotton cloth. In Dalton, the Crane Paper Company produced the special paper used to make the nation's money. Factories in Lynn, Worcester, and Marlborough made shoes and boots for the entire country. Many factory employees were women and children who worked long hours in difficult conditions for very little pay.

Wars and Peace

Industrialized states in the North contrasted with those in the South, where agriculture was the main industry. Another issue, slavery, eventually divided the two regions even further. On the plantations of the South, most of the hard labor was done by African-American slaves.

Massachusetts was the first slaveholding New England colony, but it had abolished (ended) slavery by 1783. Other Northern states subsequently abolished slavery as well. Like other Northern states, Massachusetts had an abolitionist (or antislavery) movement, dedicated to ending slavery nationwide. Many people say the movement began in 1831, when William Lloyd Garrison first published

The Fifty-Fourth Massachusetts Regiment was one of the first African-American regiments in the United States.

his antislavery newspaper, the *Liberator*, in Boston. Eventually, the differences between North and South led eleven Southern states to secede (withdraw) from the United States. The Civil War (1861–1865) was fought to keep the nation together.

When the Civil War broke out, Massachusetts quickly answered President Abraham Lincoln's call to arms. The state sent the first troops into battle. Military units from Massachusetts included the Fifty-Fourth Massachusetts Regiment, one of the first African-American regiments in the country. Those who remained at home went to work in factories making guns, ammunition, ships, tents, blankets, and bandages. After the South was defeated and the Civil War ended, the Thirteenth Amendment to the U.S. Constitution abolished slavery throughout the United States.

In the 1840s, thousands of immigrants came to Massachusetts to escape a severe famine in Ireland. In the later decades of the nineteenth century, people from many different countries poured into Massachusetts looking for work. Immigrants from France, Italy, Poland, Ireland, Portugal, Germany, and Greece joined immigrants from Finland, Latvia, Lithuania, and Turkey in seeking a better life in the commonwealth. Many of these workers had valuable skills, and because of them, Massachusetts prospered. This era of progress, known as the Industrial Age, lasted through the outbreak of World War I.

When America entered World War I in 1917, many Massachusetts citizens enlisted to fight for their country. Others stayed at home, building guns and ships and manufacturing other supplies. After the war ended, telephones, automobiles, electricity, and other new conveniences rapidly improved daily life.

Then, in 1929, the stock market crashed and everything changed. During the period known as the Great Depression, people lost their jobs, businesses closed,

As the men of Massachusetts left to fight in World War I, the state's women stepped up to fill their roles at home.

During World War II, Massachusetts's factories, such as this General Electric plant, manufactured parts for U.S. warships.

and banks failed. Few people escaped hardship. The federal government took many steps to strengthen the economy, and in time, things began to turn around. When World War II broke out in Europe in 1939, once again, Massachusetts's skilled workers were needed. By 1941, the United States had entered the war, and Massachusetts's factories were busy producing wartime goods.

After the war, Massachusetts continued to grow. Boston became an international trading city. Workers found new jobs in medicine and technology. Scientists and researchers made exciting discoveries at colleges and universities and in hospital laboratories throughout the state. New immigrants from Asia, Latin America, and the Caribbean settled in Massachusetts and added to the rich mix of cultures and ideas. Over the years, people in Massachusetts have taken great pride in their state's leading place in the country and in the world.

Important Dates

★ **1500s** Algonquians, including the Nipmuc, Nauset, Patuxet, and Wampanoag tribes, live in the region.

★ **1614** English captain John Smith maps the coast of northern New England.

★ **1620** The Pilgrims settle in Plymouth.

★ **1628** The first Puritan settlers arrive in Massachusetts.

★ **1675–1676** Colonists fight American Indians in King Philip's War.

★ **1692** The Salem witchcraft trials take place.

★ **1770** British soldiers open fire on colonists in the Boston Massacre.

★ **1773** The Boston Tea Party takes place.

★ **1775** The American Revolution begins at Lexington and Concord.

★ **1776** The Declaration of Independence is adopted.

★ **1788** Massachusetts becomes the sixth state to ratify the U.S. Constitution.

★ **1806** The African Meeting House, the nation's first African-American church, is built in Boston.

★ **1831** William Lloyd Garrison founds the antislavery publication the *Liberator*.

★ **1861–1865** The Civil War is fought.

★ **1891** The first game of basketball is played in Springfield.

★ **1912** The Bread and Roses labor strike takes place in Lawrence.

★ **1939–1945** World War II is fought.

★ **1960** John F. Kennedy of Massachusetts is elected U.S. president.

★ **1974** After a court order, Boston begins busing to integrate schools.

★ **2004** The Boston Red Sox win baseball's World Series for the first time since 1918.

★ **2007** Deval Patrick, the first African-American governor of Massachusetts, takes office.

The People

Massachusetts is filled with people who have come from, or whose ancestors have come from, all over the world. These people of diverse backgrounds bring their own traditions and learn about those of others. Together, they make Massachusetts an exciting and interesting place to live.

Massachusetts ranks forty-fifth among the states in size , but as of 2007, it ranked fourteenth in population. Only two states—New Jersey and Rhode Island—have denser populations. (Population density refers to the number of people per square mile or square kilometer.) Today, almost half of all Bay Staters live in towns, cities, and suburbs within 50 miles (80 km) of Boston.

A Cultural Bean Pot

After the American Indian population shrank, English settlers became the most powerful group in Massachusetts. For centuries, the families who traced their beginnings in America to the *Mayflower*, such as the Cabot, Lodge, Adams, Emerson, and Lowell

In Their Own Words

Here's to dear old Boston,
The home of the bean and the cod,

Where Lowells speak only to Cabots

And Cabots speak only to God.

—John Collins Bossidy,
Boston poet

Tourists and residents walk in front of Boston's historic Faneuil Hall.

The St. Patrick's Day Parade in South Boston always draws a huge crowd.

families, dominated the culture of the commonwealth. For the most part, this hardworking, reserved group of people, often called Yankees, represented the Massachusetts way of life to the world.

Then, in the 1840s, Irish immigrants came in great numbers to escape Ireland's potato famine. The Yankees felt threatened by the Irish immigrants and tried to keep them from going to public events. They even posted "No Irish Need Apply" signs to keep the new arrivals from getting jobs. Today, however, Irish Americans are the state's largest ethnic group and are very active in the state's politics, society, and trade.

After the Irish came ashore, people from Germany, Russia, Poland, Portugal, Italy, Greece, and French Canada immigrated to Massachusetts. These eager newcomers settled in the many mill and factory towns and began building communities.

After the European cultures created a flavorful blend of traditions, a new ingredient was added. Since the 1970s, immigrants from the Caribbean and Asia have settled in Lowell and other cities. Often, children playing in neighborhood

This Lowell girl shows off a mehndi design on her palm. This art form from India is usually used on special occasions such as weddings and festivals.

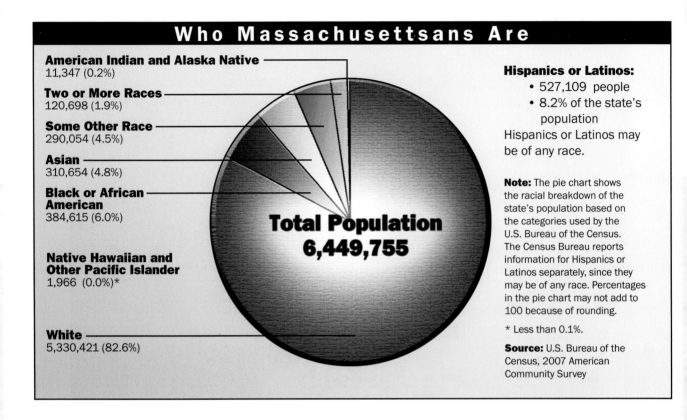

Who Massachusettsans Are

American Indian and Alaska Native
11,347 (0.2%)

Two or More Races
120,698 (1.9%)

Some Other Race
290,054 (4.5%)

Asian
310,654 (4.8%)

Black or African American
384,615 (6.0%)

Native Hawaiian and Other Pacific Islander
1,966 (0.0%)*

White
5,330,421 (82.6%)

Total Population 6,449,755

Hispanics or Latinos:
- 527,109 people
- 8.2% of the state's population

Hispanics or Latinos may be of any race.

Note: The pie chart shows the racial breakdown of the state's population based on the categories used by the U.S. Bureau of the Census. The Census Bureau reports information for Hispanics or Latinos separately, since they may be of any race. Percentages in the pie chart may not add to 100 because of rounding.

* Less than 0.1%.

Source: U.S. Bureau of the Census, 2007 American Community Survey

parks speak English to one another while at night they speak Khmer (the language of Cambodia) or Spanish to family members at home. Lowell's Cambodian community is the second largest in the nation.

Many of Boston's neighborhoods have a lively ethnic and cultural atmosphere. Its oldest neighborhood, the North End, has a rich immigrant history. Its narrow streets were laid out in the 1600s along the city's wharves. When immigrants stepped off their ships, they found it easy to move into the buildings nearby. English, Polish, Russian, Jewish, Portuguese, Irish, and Italians all made homes in this historic community. Today, the neighborhood is mostly Italian. Hispanics from the Dominican Republic, Puerto Rico, Cuba, and many other Spanish-speaking areas have contributed to the blend of cultures in neighborhoods south of Boston.

Another lively neighborhood full of shops, businesses, and restaurants is Chinatown. Many people of Chinese, Japanese, Korean, Cambodian, and

Vietnamese backgrounds live and work there. "I think we should call it Asian Town," says one community leader.

People have come to live in Massachusetts for many reasons, but they all have come hoping for a fresh start. As one lifelong resident asks, "Why would anyone want to be anywhere else?"

The Chinese New Year is an important—and exciting—celebration in the Chinatown area of Boston.

Famous Bay Staters

Lucy Stone: Women's Rights Advocate

Lucy Stone was born in 1818 in West Brookfield. In 1847, she became one of the first Massachusetts women to earn a college degree. When Stone was asked to write a speech for her college commencement, she refused. Women were not allowed to give public addresses at the time, and she had no interest in hearing a man read her speech. Stone played major roles in the abolitionist and women's rights movements. In fact, she organized the first convention on women's rights—in Worcester, Massachusetts, in 1850—that brought together participants from all over the United States.

Louisa May Alcott: Author

Louisa May Alcott was born in Pennsylvania in 1832 but lived most of her life in Boston and Concord. Writing was an early passion for Alcott, who published her first book in 1854. When Alcott was thirty-five years old, her publisher asked her to write a book for girls. *Little Women*, a huge success at the time of its printing, remains an American classic. Alcott wrote more than thirty books and story collections before her death in 1888.

William Edward Burghardt Du Bois: Educator and Writer

W. E. B. Du Bois was born in Great Barrington in 1868. In 1890, he graduated from Harvard, and five years later, he became the first African American to earn a doctoral degree from the university. Du Bois was a cofounder of the NAACP (National Association for the Advancement of Colored People) and wrote more than twenty books. Du Bois felt strongly that higher education was the key to success. He devoted himself to the cause of equal educational opportunity at a time when few African Americans went to college.

Theodor Geisel (Dr. Seuss): Children's Author

Nearly every American today has read the books of Theodor Geisel, who was born in Springfield in 1904. Geisel, who called himself Dr. Seuss, wrote and illustrated some of the most clever, entertaining children's books ever written. Geisel's publisher once bet the author fifty dollars that he could not write a book using only fifty words. The result was the classic children's favorite *Green Eggs and Ham*.

The Kennedy Brothers: Politicians

One of America's most famous political clans is the Kennedy family of Massachusetts. John Fitzgerald Kennedy (JFK) was the second son of millionaire Joseph P. Kennedy Sr. and his wife, Rose. JFK was a World War II hero who was elected president of the United States in 1960. He was assassinated in 1963. Five years later, his younger brother Robert, a U.S. senator, was also killed by an assassin's bullet. Youngest brother Edward (Ted) was a U.S. senator from 1962 until his death in 2009. Some of the Kennedy brothers' children have also gone into politics. Other family members have worked for causes such as the environment, international human rights, children's health, and supporting the disabled and the poor.

Matt Damon: Actor

Actor Matt Damon was born in 1970 in Cambridge, where he also grew up. He studied English at Harvard for three years before leaving to pursue a film career. Damon has starred in many major movies, including *The Bourne Identity* and its sequels and *Good Will Hunting*, which he cowrote with friend (and fellow Bay Stater) Ben Affleck. Damon and Affleck won the Academy Award for Best Original Screenplay for the film in 1997.

The Commonwealth of Learning

Higher education has been the soul of Massachusetts since the 1600s. Harvard University, founded in 1636, was the first institution of higher learning in what would become the United States. Later, in the nineteenth century, many other major colleges and universities were established in Massachusetts. In or near the capital city are Boston University, Brandeis University, Northeastern University, Boston College, and the Massachusetts Institute of Technology (MIT). Farther west are Williams College, Clark University, Amherst College, the University of Massachusetts, and the Worcester Polytechnic Institute. Women's colleges such as Radcliffe (now part of Harvard), Smith, Mount Holyoke, and Wellesley were

Harvard University, founded in Cambridge as Harvard College in 1636, is one of the most respected educational institutions in the world.

founded in the late nineteenth century. Because many Massachusetts residents are so well educated, the Bay State has long been at the leading edge of ideas and achievements.

Massachusetts was the first state in the nation to require all children to attend public school. But not all schools were equal. Throughout most of the country's history, many schools in the United States were segregated. White children and black children went to different schools. In many Southern states, laws and government policies established totally separate school systems for white children and black children. In many states, including Massachusetts, this was not the case. However, African-American families tended to live in different neighborhoods, so their children went to different schools. The schools for African-American children often had inferior facilities and out-of-date textbooks. In 1954, in a case called *Brown v. Board of Education of Topeka, Kansas*, the U.S. Supreme Court ruled that segregated schools violated the U.S. Constitution. Still, many states were slow to integrate their school systems.

In 1965, more than ten years after the *Brown* ruling, Boston schools were still largely segregated, and schools in black neighborhoods tended to be inferior to those in white areas of the city. With the help of the NAACP, black parents complained to the Boston School Committee. However, Louise Hicks, the committee chair, claimed the black schools were not inferior. "A racially imbalanced school," she said, "is not educationally harmful."

After years of trying to change the situation, black parents in Boston finally took their case to court. In 1974, a federal district court judge ordered the schools to integrate. To achieve a balance of black students and white students, children were bused to schools in different parts of the city. Many white people opposed busing. In September, buses carrying black students in South Boston

> ## In Their Own Words
>
> *Genius without education is like silver in the mine.*
>
> —Boston-born statesman Benjamin Franklin

African-American students travel under police escort in 1974 during Boston's school integration crisis.

Today, parents, educators, and government leaders work to ensure that all children have access to quality education in Massachusetts.

were met by angry mobs throwing rocks. Some white parents even pulled their children out of school. The resistance to busing and the violent behavior continued for years. The situation finally settled down after Hicks was replaced as committee chair and a black person was elected to the committee.

Almost a decade before forced busing in Boston, the voluntary busing METCO (Metropolitan Council for Educational Opportunity) program began sending inner-city students to suburban schools. More than three thousand students currently participate in the program. More than five times that number are on a waiting list, hoping they will get the chance to earn a quality education. Some people argue that instead of spending money on busing, the government should invest in improving inner-city schools. Others fear that this would eventually lead back to fully segregated schools. Unlike forty years ago, however, advocates on both sides are focused on the welfare of the children.

Calendar of Events

★ **Chinese New Year**

On the lunar New Year, which falls in January or February, thousands of people gather in Boston's Chinatown to watch costumed lion dances and fireworks. Following tradition, many decorate their doorways in red and give children gifts of money in red-and-gold envelopes.

★ **Patriots' Day and the Boston Marathon**

On the third Monday in April, citizens gather in Boston and nearby towns to watch reenactments of Paul Revere's ride and of the battles of Lexington and Concord. Later, they line the streets to cheer on thousands of runners in the world's oldest annual marathon.

★ **Dragon Boat Festival**

In June, Asian Americans sponsor the Charles River Dragon Boat Festival. The longest-running dragon boat festival in North America includes dancing, music, drumming, martial arts demonstrations, plenty of Asian food, and—of course—races featuring beautifully carved wooden boats.

★ **Boston Pops Fourth of July**

On the Fourth of July, the Boston Pops Orchestra gives a rousing patriotic concert along the banks of the Charles River under a sky full of fireworks.

★ **Mashpee Powwow**

In July, visitors are invited to Mashpee, on Cape Cod, where Wampanoags host their annual powwow. Tribal members perform traditional dances, songs, drumming, and storytelling and serve a feast of lobster, quahogs (clams), strawberries, and corn bread.

★ Feast of the Blessed Sacrament

In midsummer, New Bedford hosts the largest Portuguese festival in the world. Visitors celebrate Portuguese culture with a special Catholic Mass and barbequed beef called *carne d'espeto*.

★ "The Big E" (Eastern States Exposition)

New England's largest fair is held every September at the Eastern States Exposition Fairgrounds in West Springfield. More than one million visitors enjoy agricultural events, arts and crafts, horse shows, farm animal and pet competitions, and musical performances.

★ Head of the Charles Regatta

In October, more than seven thousand competitors race on Boston's Charles River in the world's largest two-day rowing event.

★ America's Hometown Thanksgiving Celebration

On the weekend before Thanksgiving, Plymouth hosts a huge celebration featuring a parade, a food fest, a craft pavilion, and concerts.

★ First Night

One of the country's largest New Year's Eve celebrations is held in Boston. The family-friendly celebration of community and the arts includes theater, music, dance, ice sculptures, laser shows, fireworks, and a First Night Grand Procession.

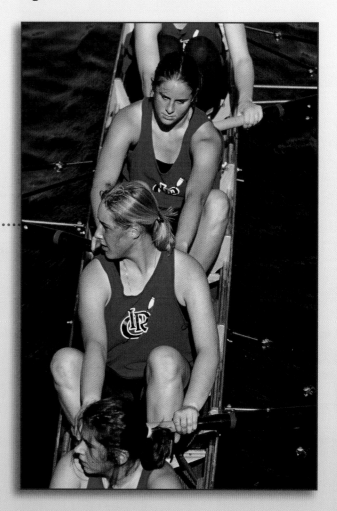

How the Government Works

On February 4, 1788, Massachusetts became the sixth state to ratify the U.S. Constitution. Its state constitution, called the Constitution of the Commonwealth of Massachusetts, is even older than the national government's. Adopted in 1780, it is the oldest state constitution still in use. Many amendments have been added, but the document that sets out how the state government operates has not been fundamentally changed in more than two hundred years.

The elegant State House in Boston is the center of Massachusetts government. But that is not the only place to find the government of Massachusetts at work. As the former speaker of the

Quick Facts

THE ROAD TO THE WHITE HOUSE

Five U.S. presidents have come from Massachusetts. John Adams was the nation's first vice president and the second president; his son John Quincy was the sixth president. Massachusetts governor Calvin Coolidge was elected vice president in 1920 and became president upon the death of President Warren Harding. John F. Kennedy, the first and only Catholic president, was elected in 1960. Massachusetts is also the birthplace of George H. W. Bush, who was elected president in 1988.

The Massachusetts State House is located on Beacon Hill across from the Boston Common.

Branches of Government

EXECUTIVE ★ ★ ★ ★ ★ ★ ★ ★ ★

The governor, lieutenant governor, and other executive officers are elected to four-year terms. The governor, who is the head of state and commander-in-chief of the state's militia (army), prepares the state budget, suggests new laws, and appoints judges and other department heads. The governor also has the power to sign bills into law or veto (refuse to sign) them.

LEGISLATIVE ★ ★ ★ ★ ★ ★ ★ ★

The state house of representatives and state senate make up Massachusetts's legislature, which is called the General Court. The senate has 40 members, and the house of representatives has 160. Senators and representatives are elected to two-year terms. Legislators propose and pass the laws that are ultimately sent to the governor for signature.

JUDICIAL ★ ★ ★ ★ ★ ★ ★ ★

The state has a system of courts made up of a supreme judicial court, a court of appeals, and many trial courts. The supreme judicial court is the highest court in the commonwealth. Most cases start in a trial court. If there is a disagreement with a trial-court ruling, the case may be heard by a court of appeals. Cases may be further appealed to the supreme judicial court. This court tends to hear only cases that raise important legal questions, including whether a law follows or violates the state constitution.

U.S. House of Representatives, Massachusetts congressman Thomas P. "Tip" O'Neill Jr., once said, "All politics is local." The government of Massachusetts starts with every citizen. Anyone, of any age, can propose a law, and any U.S. citizen eighteen or older who lives in Massachusetts can register to vote in local, state, and federal elections.

There are three levels of government in Massachusetts: city or town; county; and state. There are fourteen counties, which are run by county commissioners. As in other New England states, county government is not very strong and has no authority to tax citizens. City dwellers elect mayors and city-council members to govern. Towns elect selectmen. Citizens and their elected officials regularly come together to discuss issues at town meetings, a tradition dating to colonial times. People can also write to their elected leaders to share concerns and

Governor Deval Patrick speaks during a town meeting in 2008. This kind of gathering gives ordinary citizens a chance to have their say.

opinions. At the highest level of state government, voters elect state senators and representatives, a governor, and other executive officeholders.

As of 2010, there were ten Massachusetts representatives in the U.S. House of Representatives. Like all states, Massachusetts has two U.S. senators in Washington, D.C. Edward "Ted" Kennedy was the fourth-longest-serving U.S. senator. He was first elected to represent Massachusetts in 1962 at the age of thirty. His career in the Senate spanned four decades, until his death in 2009.

Contacting Lawmakers

★ ★ ★ ★ ★ ★ ★ ★ ★ ★ ★ ★ ★

You can e-mail Massachusetts state legislators or look up their names, addresses, and telephone numbers at

www.mass.gov/legis

In that time, he became one of the U.S. Senate's most influential members.

The United States has two major parties: the Democratic Party and the Republican Party. Ted Kennedy, who was known as "the lion of the Senate," was respected for his ability to "reach across the aisle." He worked well with Republicans as well as members of his own party.

After Kennedy's death, a special election in 2010 determined who would finish out his term in the U.S. Senate. Republican Scott Brown ran against

An important part of a governor's job is signing bills into law. Governor Deval Patrick signs a transportation reform bill in 2009.

Democrat Martha Coakley and won. Massachusetts had a Republican U.S. senator for the first time in more than three decades.

The state's other senator is Democrat John Kerry. He ran for president in 2004 against George W. Bush and lost. He won his bid for reelection to the U.S. Senate in 2008.

How a Bill Becomes a Law

The commonwealth has more state symbols than most states. It has a state muffin (corn), a state historical rock (Plymouth), and even a state bean (navy, as the original Boston baked bean). The story of how one symbol, the state insect, was chosen shows how laws are passed in Massachusetts.

One day in 1974 at Kennedy Elementary School in Franklin, Massachusetts, second-grade teacher Palma Johnson told her class about official state symbols. Her students asked why there was a state tree, bird, and fish but no state insect. They decided the ladybug would make an excellent state symbol and that they should try to make it official. The students learned that anyone living in Massachusetts could ask to have a law passed. First they needed a special form called a petition, as well as a legislator to sign it. So the children wrote to their representative, who agreed to sign their petition.

After that, there was much work to do. First the petition had to become a bill. It was given an identification number—House Bill 5155—and sent to a committee, which discussed whether the legislators should vote on it. Johnson's students went to the State House in Boston to explain why the ladybug should be the official state insect. They told the legislators, "They're so beautiful with their shiny orange backs and bold black spots, and they can be found in everyone's backyard."

The committee agreed with the students and presented the bill to the entire house of representatives. The representatives needed to talk about the bill three times before they could vote on it. The class visited or wrote letters to members of the house, asking them to vote for the bill. After the three discussions, the representatives voted to make the ladybug the official state insect.

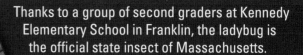

Thanks to a group of second graders at Kennedy Elementary School in Franklin, the ladybug is the official state insect of Massachusetts.

In order to become a law, the bill had to go to the senate. The children returned to the State House, this time to the senate chamber. They asked for and received the senators' votes. The bill was very nearly a law. First it was printed on special paper called parchment and delivered to the governor. If the governor signed it, the bill would be a law. If the governor vetoed it, the bill would not be a law. The governor did sign the bill, and the ladybug became the official state insect of Massachusetts.

The Law of the Land

The state legislature has the power to make laws. The judicial system has a powerful role in how the state's laws are interpreted. The courts are responsible for deciding whether state laws are legal under the Massachusetts constitution. If a law does not agree with the constitution, the supreme judicial court can declare that law unconstitutional. A famous case argued in Massachusetts in the late 1700s illustrates how this works. An enslaved woman named Elizabeth Freeman brought the case to court.

Freeman's owner, Colonel John Ashley, was very involved in Massachusetts politics and government. While serving her owner and his political friends at the table, Freeman listened carefully to their conversations. The men discussed many issues of the day, including the new Massachusetts constitution.

One day, the colonel's wife tried to beat Freeman's sister. Freeman was furious. She marched through cold, icy weather to the home of Theodore Sedgwick, a lawyer who she knew did not believe in slavery. Freeman asked

Among other things, Massachusetts courts help determine whether laws are constitutional. This hearing takes place at the Massachusetts Supreme Judicial Court in Boston.

why the new constitution did not protect her and her sister. Yet the men at Colonel Ashley's dinner table were always talking about all people being "born free and equal."

Sedgwick agreed to take Freeman's case before a judge, where he argued that the law permitting slavery was unconstitutional. The judge agreed, saying that the true meaning of the 1780 state constitution clearly was that "all men are born free and equal." The judge ruled that Elizabeth Freeman and her sister were free—and slavery in Massachusetts was soon abolished.

Making a Living

The economy of Massachusetts has changed a great deal over the past almost four hundred years. When the area was first settled by people from England, colonists made their living off the land. In addition to foreign trade, the base of Massachusetts's economy was formed by fishing and farming. These industries have shrunk dramatically over the years, however. Less than one percent of the state's workforce is engaged in these industries today. Manufacturing became a major part of the state's economy in the 1800s after Francis Cabot Lowell built his power loom. But in recent decades, manufacturing has declined. After World War II, computers and technology took on new importance. This "new economy" continues to be at the core of Massachusetts's economy, as do the service and tourism industries.

Fishing and Farming

In the late 1700s and early 1800s, fishing—and whaling—contributed greatly to the state's pocketbook. When the New Bedford whaling boom reached its peak in 1857, more than three hundred vessels were sailing out of the port. The fleet, worth more than $12 million, employed ten thousand men. By the early 1900s, however, the whaling industry in America was virtually dead. Today, whale populations off the coast of Massachusetts contribute to the state economy in a much less gruesome way. According to the World Wildlife Fund, the Bay State

Boston's New England Aquarium attracts
more than one million visitors a year.

A DEAD WHALE
OR A
STOVE BOAT

is one of the top-ten whale-watching spots in the world.

New England's fishing industry has always been tied to groundfishing—catching bottom-dwelling fish such as cod and haddock. The 1970s saw a decline in the industry due to overfishing and pollution. The state has made a comeback, however, and Massachusetts now ranks third in the country for the economic impact of its fishing industry.

This statue, created in 1913 by Bela Lyon Pratt, commemorates New Bedford's whaling industry.

Quick Facts

STUDYING THE SEA

In the seaside village of Woods Hole on Cape Cod is a world center for oceanographic research and marine biology. Scientists from around the world study fish, aquatic plants and animals, whales, the ocean floor, ecosystems, and climate change. Woods Hole Oceanographic Institution is also the home of *Alvin*, the submersible (small submarine) that explored the wreck of the *Titanic*.

Workers & Industries

Industry	Number of People Working in That Industry	Percentage of All Workers Who Are Working in That Industry
Education and health care	844,344	25.8%
Wholesale and retail businesses	444,303	13.5%
Professionals, scientists, and managers	419,546	12.8%
Publishing, media, entertainment, hotels, and restaurants	361,303	11.0%
Manufacturing	318,326	9.7%
Banking and finance, insurance, and real estate	279,025	8.5%
Construction	199,273	6.1%
Other services	144,611	4.4%
Government	128,533	3.9%
Transportation and public utilities	123,265	3.8%
Farming, fishing, forestry, and mining	14,580	0.4%
Totals	**3,277,109**	**100%**

Notes: Figures above do not include people in the armed forces. "Professionals" includes people such as doctors and lawyers. Percentages may not add to 100 because of rounding.

Source: U.S. Bureau of the Census, 2007 estimates

Although fewer Massachusettsans work in farming than any other industry, the Bay State is still home to thousands of farms. In 2009, the value of agricultural production—crop and livestock sales—was almost $500 million. In southeastern Massachusetts, farmers grow about 30 percent of the country's cranberry crop. The tart red berry is one of the few truly native American fruits. Algonquian tribes used it for food and medicine and as a dye for blankets and rugs.

A farmer harvests cranberries in Carver.

RECIPE FOR CRANBERRY SAUCE

Cranberries are an important crop in Massachusetts. With the help of an adult, you can make delicious cranberry sauce using this recipe.

WHAT YOU NEED

4 cups (about 1 liter) frozen or fresh cranberries

1 cup (230 ml) water

$\frac{3}{4}$ cup (150 grams) sugar

If you are using fresh cranberries, be sure to wash them well. Frozen cranberries should be defrosted at room temperature before using.

With the help of an adult, boil the water and sugar in a saucepan on the stove. Be sure to stir the sugar as it dissolves. Add the cranberries and bring to a boil. Reduce the heat to low and simmer until the cranberries burst and break apart, 8 to 10 minutes.

Let the sauce cool until it reaches room temperature, and then refrigerate until ready to use.

Serve your delicious cranberry sauce with turkey, chicken, or pork, or use it as a topping for bread, croissants, or other pastries.

JOHNNY APPLESEED
Massachusetts folk hero John "Johnny Appleseed" Chapman was born in Leominster in 1774. As settlers began to push west, Chapman saw a need for apple trees along the frontier. He set out from Massachusetts on foot, selling or giving away apple seeds that he had bought from cider mills. Over the course of his travels, Johnny Appleseed planted seeds in western Pennsylvania, Ohio, Indiana, Illinois, and Kentucky. Many folk stories feature the Johnny Appleseed character.

Manufacturing

After Lowell introduced his power loom in the 1800s, textile manufacturing contributed a great deal to the economy of Massachusetts. Factories in the state also turned out shoes, leather goods, paper, lumber for building, printed goods, ships, tools, and games. Most of the original factories have shut down, but new ones have taken their places. Almost 10 percent of Bay Staters work in factories manufacturing electrical and industrial equipment, technical instruments, plastic products, paper and paper products, machinery, tools, and metal and rubber goods.

Scientists at the Massachusetts Institute of Technology (MIT) worked with the U.S. Navy in the 1940s on a project that led to the design of a high-speed digital computer. And, in 1971, the world's first e-mail was sent from a computer in Cambridge. Now, Route 128—the highway that circles Boston, Lexington, and Cambridge—links technology companies and major universities. Together they develop products and ideas that benefit the entire world.

Researchers at MIT began working on Whirlwind, a large-scale, general-purpose computer, in 1944. It took several years to become operational.

Cranberries

Massachusetts is the second-largest cranberry-producing state, after Wisconsin. Farmers produce about 2 million barrels of this colorful fruit each year. Most cranberry farms are in the southeastern part of the state, where saltwater bogs and wetlands make for an ideal growing environment.

Apples

McIntosh, Cortland, pippin, and New England Red Delicious are among the many varieties of apples grown in the state. Most of the more than one hundred apple orchards are family farms.

Horticulture

Horticulture—growing fruits, vegetables, flowers, shrubs, and trees—has long been a part of the Massachusetts economy. Landscape plants for home gardens and lawns are the major horticultural crop in the state. In 1852, a Concord horticulturist bred a grape from different native varieties. He called it the "grape for the millions." Today Concord grapes are used in juices, jams, and sweeteners around the world.

Fishing

The Massachusetts fishing industry has seen better days, but fishing is still part of coastal life. From New Bedford to Newburyport, fishers catch haddock, cod, and halibut using gillnets, longlines, or dragging gear. Others harvest lobsters and scallops.

Printing

The Boston-area economy has relied on printing, publishing, and bookbinding for more than a century. The very first printing press in the nation was used at the Cambridge Press, founded in 1639. James Franklin (Benjamin Franklin's brother) started the *New England Courant*, the first newspaper to include local news and opinion pieces, in Boston in 1721. (Benjamin worked as his older brother's apprentice.)

Tourism

The commonwealth's third-largest industry is tourism. It employs more than 125,000 people and generates more than $887 million in revenue each year. One popular tourist attraction is the swan boats in Boston Public Garden.

Fun and Games

Massachusetts is home to some of the best-known teams in sports—and some of the most fanatical fans. The Boston Red Sox have been playing baseball in historic Fenway Park since 1912. After an eighty-six-year drought (some people said the team was cursed), the Sox won the World Series in 2004 and again in 2007. The Boston Celtics, the city's professional basketball team, has won seventeen NBA titles over its storied history. That is more than any other team in the league. The New England Patriots call Foxborough's Gillette Stadium home. In 2005, the Pats became only the second team in NFL history to win three Super Bowls in four years. (They took home the trophy in Super Bowl XXXVI, XXXVIII, and XXXIX.)

Fans watch a Red Sox game from left field at Fenway Park.

An estimated 500 million people worldwide have played Monopoly since its creation in 1935.

A GAMING HISTORY

Milton Bradley started manufacturing games and puzzles in the late 1800s. For years, the Milton Bradley factory in East Longmeadow produced family favorites such as Candy Land, the Game of Life, Twister, and Scrabble. George Parker, of Parker Brothers fame, was born in Salem. With brothers Charles and Edward, he began selling Monopoly in 1935. It remains one of the world's most popular games.

A family enjoys the impressive autumn colors of the Berkshires.

Tourism

It is not surprising that a state as rich in history and natural attractions as Massachusetts has a thriving tourism industry. Every year, millions of people visit the Bay State to walk the Freedom Trail, a 2.5-mile (4-km) walking path that includes sixteen historic sites. Stops along the trail include the site of the Boston Massacre, Paul Revere's house, and Faneuil Hall. It is sometimes called the Cradle of Liberty because of its association with revolutionary colonists such as Samuel Adams.

Visitors to Massachusetts also enjoy fine dining, world-class museums, and cultural events. They experience the best Mother Nature has to offer in every season. The Berkshire Mountains are bursting with color during fall foliage time. In the winter, there is skiing, snowboarding, and other cold-weather activities. In summertime, people from all over the country flock to Cape Cod and beautiful Nantucket Island, where they might visit the quaint towns, go on a whale-watching trip, or relax on the beach.

In 2008, the total number of people visiting Massachusetts from other states or other countries (including vacationers and people traveling for business) was more than 19 million. They helped provide jobs for the thousands of Bay Staters who work in hotels, restaurants, stores, tourist sites, and other service businesses.

State Flag & Seal

The state flag of Massachusetts features the coat of arms of the commonwealth—showing an American Indian holding a bow and arrow, with the arrow pointing downward to indicate that the Indian is peaceful. The background and a star in the coat of arms are white. The state motto is written in Latin on a ribbon beneath the coat of arms. The motto translates to "By the Sword We Seek Peace, but Peace Only Under Liberty."

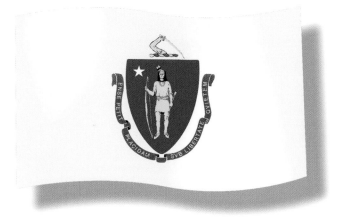

The Massachusetts state seal also features the commonwealth's coat of arms. The star (silver instead of white) indicates that Massachusetts was one of the thirteen original colonies. The state seal was made official on June 4, 1885.

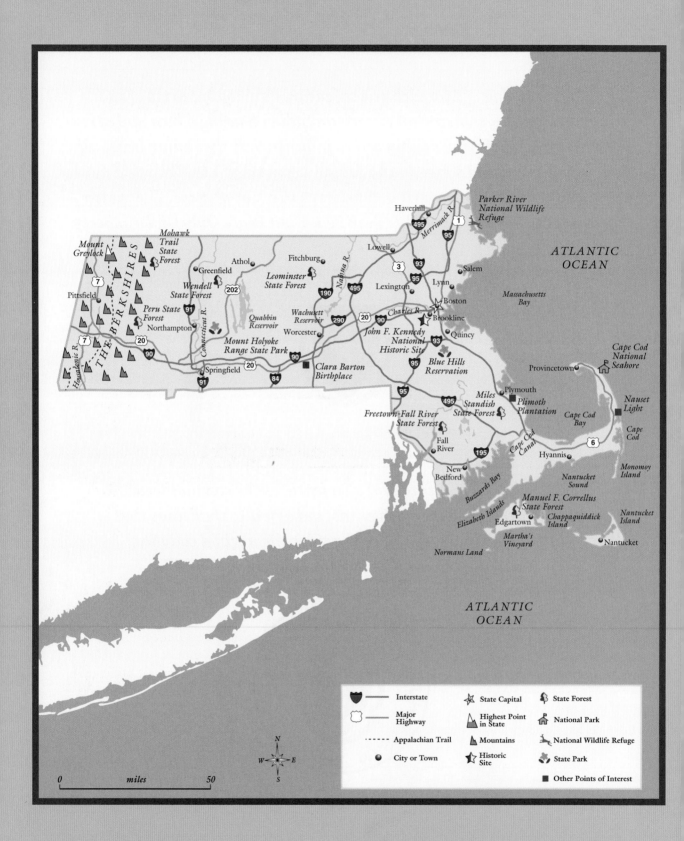

ATLANTIC
OCEAN

Parker River
National Wildlife
Refuge

Haverhill

Merrimack R.

THE BERKSHIRES

Mount
Greylock

Mohawk
Trail
State
Forest

Athol

Fitchburg

Lowell

Salem

Massachusetts
Bay

Pittsfield

Greenfield

Wendell
State
Forest

Leominster
State Forest

Nashua R.

Lexington

Lynn

Peru State
Forest

Northampton

Quabbin
Reservoir

Wachusett
Reservoir

Worcester

Charles R.

Boston

Brookline

John F. Kennedy
National
Historic Site

Quincy

Cape Cod
National
Seashore

Mount Holyoke
Range State Park

Springfield

Clara Barton
Birthplace

Blue Hills
Reservation

Provincetown

Nauset
Light

Freetown-Fall River
State Forest

Miles
Standish
State Forest

Plymouth

Plimoth
Plantation

Cape Cod
Bay

Cape
Cod

Fall
River

Hyannis

Cape Cod Canal

New
Bedford

Buzzards Bay

Nantucket
Sound

Monomoy
Island

Elizabeth Islands

Manuel F. Correllus
State Forest

Chappaquiddick
Island

Nantucket
Island

Edgartown

Martha's
Vineyard

Nantucket

Normans Land

ATLANTIC
OCEAN

Connecticut R.

Housatonic R.

	Interstate		State Capital		State Forest
	Major Highway		Highest Point in State		National Park
	Appalachian Trail		Mountains		National Wildlife Refuge
	City or Town		Historic Site		State Park
					Other Points of Interest

N
W   E
S

0   miles   50

State Song

All Hail to Massachusetts

words and music by Arthur J. Marsh

BOOKS

Arenstam, Peter Harper, John Kemp, and Catherine O'Neill Grace. *Mayflower 1620: A New Look at a Pilgrim Voyage*. Washington, DC: National Geographic Children's Books, 2007.

Decker, Timothy. *For Liberty: The Story of the Boston Massacre*. Honesdale, PA: Front Street, 2009.

Fradin, Dennis B. *The Boston Tea Party*. New York: Marshall Cavendish Benchmark, 2007.

Fradin, Judith Bloom, and Dennis B. Fradin. *The Salem Witch Trials*. New York: Marshall Cavendish Children's Books, 2009.

Levy, Janey. *The Wampanoag of Massachusetts and Rhode Island*. New York: PowerKids Press, 2005.

McElroy, Lisa Tucker. *Ted Kennedy: A Remarkable Life in the Senate*. Minneapolis: Lerner Publications, 2009.

WEBSITES

The Freedom Trail:
http://www.thefreedomtrail.org

New England Aquarium:
http://www.neaq.org

The Official Massachusetts Government Page:
http://www.mass.gov

Old Sturbridge Village:
http://www.osv.org

Plimoth Plantation:
http://www.plimoth.org

Ruth Bjorklund has written a number of books for young readers on topics ranging from states to animals to health issues. She has lived in the Berkshires, in Boston, and on Cape Cod. She is a former youth services librarian and shares her home on Bainbridge Island, Washington, with her husband, two children, and their pets.

Stephanie Fitzgerald has been writing nonfiction for children for more than ten years, and she is the author of more than twenty books. Her specialties include history, wildlife, and popular culture. She lives in Stamford, Connecticut, with her husband and their daughter.

★ INDEX ★

Page numbers in **boldface** are illustrations.

Adams, John, 31, 55
Adams, Samuel, 74
Affleck, Ben, 47
African Americans, 31, 35–36, **36**, 39, **44**, 46, **46**, 49–51, **50**, 60–61
agriculture. *See* farming
Alcott, Louisa May, 46, **46**
American Indians, 9, **20**, 21–25, **23**, **24**, 26–27, 41, **44**, 75, **75**
American Revolution, **29**, 30, **31**
animals, 4, **4**, 5, **5**, 10, 11, 14, **16**, 16–17, 18, **18**, 19, **19**, 21, 53, 59–60, **60**, **62**, 63–64, 71
    See also birds; dogs; ladybugs; whales
area, 7
Asian Americans, 38, **44**, 44–45, **45**, 52

beaches, 7, 12, **12**, 13, 16, 21, 74
birds, 10, 11, 16, **16**, 59
    state bird, 5, **5**
boats, 14, 15, 19, 52, **53**, 71, **71**
borders, 7
Boston, 7, 10, 11, 14, **15**, 25, 28, **28**, 30, 35–36, 38, 39, **40**, 41, **42**, 44–45, **45**, 46, 48, 49–51, **50**, 52, **52**, 53, **53**, **54**, 55, 59, **61**, **62**, 68, 71, **71**, 72, **72**, 74
Boston Massacre, 28, 74
Boston Tea Party, 28, **28**
Bread and Roses strike, 35
Brown, Scott, 58–59
Bush, George H. W., 14, 55
Bush, George W., 59

Cambridge, 4, 47, **48**, 68

candle-making project, 32–33
Cape Cod, 11, **12**, 12–13, **13**, 16, 22, 23, 52, 64, 74
capital. *See* Boston
Chapman, John "Johnny Appleseed," 68, **68**
children, 35, 42–44, **43**, 47, 49–51, **51**, 52, 59–60
Civil War, 36, **36**
computers, 63, 68, **69**
Concord, 28, 30, 46, 52, 70
Connecticut River Valley, 10
conservation, 5, 16–17, **17**, 64
cookies, 5, **5**
counties, 7, **8**, 56
courts, 26–27, 49, 56, 60–61, **61**
cranberries, 12, 66, **66**, 67, **67**, 70

Damon, Matt, 47, **47**
dams, 10, 18
dogs, 4, **4**
Du Bois, W. E. B., 46, **46**

Eastern Massachusetts, 7, 11, **11**
education, 46, **48**, 48–49, 49–51, 65
educators, 46, **46**, 59
Emerson, Ralph Waldo, 30
endangered species, 5, 14, **16**, 16–17, **17**, 18, **18**
ethnic groups, 35, 41–45, **42**, **43**, **44**
    See also African Americans; American Indians; Asian Americans; Hispanic Americans; immigrants; Irish Americans; Italian Americans
explorers, 22, **22**

Fall River, 35
farming, 9–10, 25, 26, 28, 63, 65, 66, **66**, 70
festivals and fairs, **43**, 52, 53
fishing, 11, 63–64, 65, 71
flag, state, **75**
flowers, 70
    state flower, 4
fossils, 10, 21
Franklin, Benjamin, 49, 71
Franklin, James, 71
Freeman, Elizabeth, 60–61
French and Indian War, 27

games, 68, **72**, 72–73, **73**
Garrison, William Lloyd, 35–36
Geisel, Theodor (Dr. Seuss), 47
government, **54**, 55–61, **58**, **61**, 65
governor(s), 39, 56, 57, **57**, **58**, 60
Great Depression, 37–38

health care, 65
Hispanic Americans, 44, **44**

immigrants, 37, 38, 42–45
    See also ethnic groups
Industrial Revolution, 34, 37
industries, **34**, 34–35, 37, 38, **38**, 63–64, 65, 66, **66**, 68, 71, 74
    See also fishing; manufacturing
Irish Americans, 37, 42, **42**
islands, 11, 12, 74
Italian Americans, 37, 42, 44

Kennedy, Edward "Ted," 47, 57–58
Kennedy, John F., 47, 55
Kennedy, Joseph P. Sr., 47
Kennedy, Robert, 47
Kennedy, Rose, 47
King Philip's War, 27

ladybugs, 59–60, **60**
Lawrence, 35
laws, 23, 28, 49, 56, 59–61
Lexington, 28, 30, 52, 68
lighthouses, 13, **13**
Lowell, Francis Cabot, 34, 63, 68
Lowell, 34, **34**, 42, **43**, 44

manufacturing, **34**, 34–35, 37–38, **38**, 63, 65, 68
maps, Massachusetts, **6**, **8**, **76**
Massasoit, **24**, 24–25, 27
Mayflower, the, 23, 41
mountains, 7, 9–10, **10**, 13, 74
museums, **23**, 74
music, 52, 53, 77

Native Americans. *See* American Indians
New Bedford, 35, 53, 63, **64**, 71
Newburyport, 71
New England, 7, 18, 22, 24, 35, 53, 54, 56
nickname, state, 5
North Shore, 11

O'Neill, Thomas P. "Tip" Jr., 55–56

parades, **42**, 53
Patrick, Deval, 39, **57**, **58**
Pilgrims, 11, **11**, 16, **23**, 23–25, **24**
plants, 16, 18, **18**, 19, 21, 70
See also flowers
population, state, 5, 41, **44**
prehistory, 11, 21
publishing, 65, 71
Puritans, 25–27

recipe, 67
Revere, Paul, 28, **29**, 52, 74
Revolutionary War. *See* American Revolution
rivers, 7, 10, 11, 14, 21, 28, 30, 35, 52, 53

Salem, 25, **26**, 26–27, 73
Salem witch trials, **26**, 26–27
seal, state, **75**
seasons, 12–13, 22
settlers. *See* Pilgrims; Puritans
size. *See* area
Smith, John, 22, **22**
song, state, 77

sports, 39, 52, **52**, 53, **53**, 72, **72**
Squanto, 25
statehood, 5, 31, 55
Stone, Lucy, 46

technology, 38, 63, 68
Thoreau, Henry David, 12
timeline, 39
tourism, 63, 71, **71**, 74
trees, 5, 7–8, 13, 16, 18, 19, 59, 70, **70, 74**
state tree, 4, 59

U.S. senators, 47, 56, 57–59

Washington, George, 4, 30
waterfalls, 9, **9**, 10
weather, 13–14, **14**, 19
websites, 58, 78
Western Massachusetts, 7–10, **9**, **10**, **74**
whales, 5, 18, **18**, 22, 63–64, **64**, 74
wildlife refuge, 10
women's rights, 31, 35, 46
workers, 10, **37**, 37–38, 65
World War I, 37, **37**
World War II, 38, **38**, 47, 63